Spiritual Polyamory

Spiritual Polyamory

✦

Mystic Life

iUniverse, Inc.
New York Lincoln Shanghai

Spiritual Polyamory

iUniverse, Inc.

For information address:
iUniverse, Inc.
2021 Pine Lake Road, Suite 100
Lincoln, NE 68512
www.iuniverse.com

ISBN: 0-595-30541-5

Printed in the United States of America

Contents

1

Loa: The Source of Spiritual Polyamory

"Love of all" is the phrase from which the word Loa has been created. Loa is a lofty goal. How can we love everyone? What about terrorists? What about rapists? Murderers? Why would you even want to love them? The reason you would want to love them is that it hurts to do otherwise.

When you are armored, you will not notice how it feels to see another as not worthy of love. When you become sensitive, you have no choice but to realize that anything less than love hurts. It hurts the other person, and because we are all connected it hurts you too.

The key to being able to practice Loa is understanding the difference between a person and their behavior which arises from ego. Ego is a collection of beliefs arising from fear and the illusion of separation. Often when a person "hates" another what they truly hate is ego. My ego is no better or worse than any other person's ego. Egos always arise from illusion, and are therefore all without credibility.

To hate another person because their action arises from ego is to hate yourself for anything you do that arises from ego. The very process of hating arises from the ego's false belief that hating will place you above another person.

Loa is the end of struggle. It is the beginning of lightness and peace.

Much of the writing within this book challenges monogamy. I question systems…it is part of who I am. When I am being critical of a system I am not being critical of the people within that system. To judge a person within the system of monogamy would arise from the ego within me that craves the illusion of superiority. I recognize the ego as both fragile and strong. It is fragile in that it is completely illogical. It is strong in that it has arisen from years of environmental and biological influence. However, I believe that our tendency is not our destiny. We may give the ego power but it is, at its core, empty and weak.

Poly people are often assumed to overvalue sex. However, I believe that monogamy is a system that overvalues sex, and here is why...

If you are monogamous, you are most likely okay with your lover sharing his or her love, time, understanding, compassion, forgiveness, nonjudgment and attention. The one thing you will probably not stand for is the sharing of their sexual intimacy. This implies that you value it above all else. It is the one thing you must "own" to feel safe. I challenge this belief.

I have experienced the values of monogamy, wholly and without doubt. I found that the end result was, ultimately, suffering, and that letting go of control is part of the path to freedom and wholeness.

We deeply crave unconditional love. If we do not question the "supposedly unconditional" love that carries with it the condition of sexual exclusivity, then we remain ignorant and incomplete in our understanding of what we can experience and share.

It is so clear upon a deeper examination of sexuality, that our desire to possess another's body arises not from love, but from fear. Sociobiologically speaking, we fear that "our mate" will procreate with another, thus diminishing the likelihood of our own genes being perpetuated. This primal desire to control another is a tendency which we are outgrowing since our true immortality is not achieved through procreation but is a natural outcome of existing as a spiritual being. So to go on attempting to control what others do with their body is to forget your true nature: a spirit in an ape suit. Give strength to your spirit self. Understand the tendencies of your ape suit without believing that you are a prisoner of your biology.

There are other false reasons to control another's body. You may fear being alone. Person addiction is pervasive in our world and understandable as when we are left alone we are forced to experience how we truly feel. In some ways it feels easier to pay attention to how others are experiencing themselves so that we may avoid our personal work. However, when we are able to be comfortable with ourselves, we are also much more capable of being authentic and healthy in our relationships.

Perhaps you have been conditioned to associate having a lover with having personal worth. If this is the case, you may find yourself consciously or unconsciously controlling your lover's body so they don't leave you for another person. However, in an enlightened system, why would you ever "leave" someone you loved if they accepted you unconditionally? You may spend different amounts of time with your lover in the future, but if both people involved in this relationship trust their path, they understand that whatever situation they find themselves in is perfect for their current lessons. Therefore, there is ultimately no benefit that could possibly come from trying to limit another person's behavior.

As you read this book, I ask that you define spiritual polyamory for yourself.

I define it for myself as: utilizing the philosophy of polyamory in my personal development as a human trying to realize my spiritual truth. I am working towards Loa, and feel that polyamory arises naturally from a state of loving all people. This path requires owning jealousy as it arises, accepting others as they are, developing my own sense of personal wholeness, and letting go of the belief that loving someone more means loving someone else less.

Much of the philosophy of polyamory can better be understood if you use how people "do" friendship as an analogy. Sexuality has many charged associations because the world we live in is, as a whole, sexually immature. If, instead, you think in terms of having multiple friendships, you may be able to better understand the philosophy of a spiritual approach to polyamory. For example, you can most likely appreciate that if you have a friend who makes a new friend, that doesn't have to pose a threat to the relationship you have with your friend. You want that person to be happy. You can therefore practice compersion, the opposite of jealousy, which states that you gain happiness when those you care about are more happy. This involves non-attachment to your ego's goals of having everyone to yourself. Once you are able to see how sexual possession has become an "accepted attachment" in your society, you can then introduce sexuality into the above "multiple friendship" scenario, and see how your responsibility to yourself is to release your attachments as opposed to struggling to preserve them.

If you are "poly-curious" and not quite sure how you feel, ask yourself the following as you read this book:

Does my desire for sexual intimacy with one person for the rest of my physical existence arise from personal congruence or cultural conditioning and/or fear of loneliness or abandonment or rejection? If you decide that sexual intimacy with more than one person is personally congruent for you, ask yourself: Which method of loving is ultimately a statement of my true self...serial or sustainable?

2

Polyamory, Other Love Styles and Common Ground

Polyamory is seen as very different than other "love styles" by some people. However, it does not exist in an entirely separate realm. The similarities are important to keep in mind when we examine polyamory (defined here as the openness to sexual intimacy and love with more than one person at a time).

I have been asked if polyamory is about sexuality or if it is about love. I've stated that if it were not for the element of sexuality there would be no need for a polyamory movement. In other words, sharing the body of another human being is the greatest ego challenge we face in our desire to experience unconditional love.

Polyamory questions the requirement of sexual monogamy. This may feel like a great threat to our sense of security. However, there is no greater sense of security in a relationship than knowing that your love is not threatened by the presence of more love.

Common Ground Between Polyamory and Traditional Dating
Both are explorations of emotions, intimacy and sexuality.

Common Ground Between Polyamory and Traditional Marriage
Both are explorations of connecting in a deep, meaningful way.

Common Ground Between Polyamory and Casual Dating
Both are explorations of sexuality without necessarily restricting the other person.

Common Ground Between Polyamory and Swinging
Both are explorations of sexual diversity beyond traditional limitations.

Common Ground Between Polyamory and Polygamy/Polyandry
Both are explorations of non-traditional sexual intimacy with others.

Common Ground Between Polyamory and Celibacy
Both are explorations of one's relationship with one's self.

We may be socialized to only pay attention to the *differences* between people, groups and beliefs. However, when we realize that we share common ground, we feel closer with each other, and less isolated in our quest to become who we are.

3

The Polyamorous Journey

To experience polyamory fully, one must be willing to live in the present. We have biological instincts which guide us towards grasping for security. They never work for long. True love arises out of an absence of control.

The time in which we are now living is much different from the past. When human life spans were short and the environment was harsh it may have made more sense to not expect to have the energy to love more than one person. In today's world it seems unreasonable to expect one person to meet all of your emotional needs for an entire lifetime. Instead of creating a trail of tears (a trail of ex-lovers) through serial monogamy, it seems more compassionate to allow new love to enter without needing to destroy existing love.

At this time, many polyamorous people feel alienated. It is similar to being gay/lesbian though the gay/lesbian population has had to deal with much greater discrimination and violence. Polyamorous people can learn from the gay/lesbian movement. It is important for some people to be willing to come out of the closet, and it is important to have a greater presence in the mass media. It seems that when people can see real images of polyamorous people, their fears and judgments are more likely to dissipate. Nearly all of romance and sexuality has been portrayed in a monogamous context. People who are in love with someone and fall in love with someone else are usually demonized. It is time for more expansive visions of love as in the films *French Twist, Kiss the Sky* and *Bandits*.

In my experience, most men talk quite differently when women are not present. It seems that many men who say they are monogamous would rather not be, but they don't feel like they have a choice. My understanding from female friends is that women also speak rather differently when men are not present. I'm writing in a heterosexual context because that is my frame of reference, but please understand that these are universal themes that apply to all people. The important aspect is that we have to start being honest with ourselves and others about who we are sexually. It seems that we are all becoming much more intuitive, and we will not be able to fool each other much longer about our desires, fantasies and longing for expansive love. Some people authentically want to be with just one person. There are many others, perhaps even a majority, who would rather experience romantic and sexual love with more than one person but don't see it as an option. It is time to convert our dreams into reality.

Sex in our culture has been portrayed as a form of commodity. In many ways, sex as a commodity seems related to the long term predominance of men owning the wealth in the world. Sexuality has become something which women possess that has power to it. Men often want to own and control the sexual power of women, and women have often exchanged sex for emotional security or out of a sense of obligation. There seems to be a dysfunctional game going on in which both genders have created a sad system that works for no one. In the process we have lost touch with our true sexual identity.

Men in monogamous relationships often live in fantasy, hoping that one day they will receive "permission" from their lover that will enable them to explore a ménage a trois or some other form of sexual expansiveness. They may fantasize that on a given drunken night with a wife and her friend, something intriguing might unfold. When people don't see themselves as having options, they resort to fantasy. However, it is possible to create a new kind of love in one's life in which everyone involved is living honestly and congruently. It is challenging to release our controlling ego-based tendencies, but it is possible.

We long for truth. Truth truly does set us free. While we can be truthful about most aspects of our experience, monogamy that is based upon fear and suppression creates a realm of dishonesty. It is normal to desire love and sex with more than one person. When this desire is suppressed it seems that the result is often negative. Holding back one's truth leads to resentment and frustration.

Holding back simply can not work anymore. It is too painful. By showing a willingness to enter the great unknown realm of polyamory, one can find their true self. It may feel challenging, but the rewards of being liberated from your desire to control others or suppress yourself is worth the challenge.

The remembrance that you as an individual are completely whole is crucial. If you feel dependent upon multiple partners that is just as unhealthy (if not more unhealthy) than being dependent in a monogamous relationship. Remember that love is an expansion of your wholeness, but that nobody should be treated like a "vital organ" that you need for your survival. Dependence is death.

The possessive mentality permeates the planet. It seems that many people are questioning the possessive mentality that leads to wars over the possession of land. There is often a correlation between a society's laws about the ownership of women and their tendency to exhibit aggressive, war-like actions. I believe that as we release ourselves from the possession that taints our individual relationships, a more peaceful planet will emerge.

Many people will resist polyamory because their traditional relationship "feels so good." If it feels good on a consistent basis then there will be no motivation to question it. Often there is a roller coaster of emotions and the highs of connection are contrasted by the lows of conflict and fears of abandonment. If it works, it works. If it doesn't work, don't just explain it away by thinking that you have the "wrong" partner. Instead, question the system in which you are experiencing love. Where did this system come from? Did it arise from your beliefs about who you are? It's possible that you were given your love style by your culture, which is not a reliable source of truth.

When you go beyond codependence, you will find your true self. You will know that you are able to give and receive love without conditions. You will still set boundaries and take care of yourself, but you will no longer be a prisoner to "needing" another person to act a certain way for your happiness. This way of being is headed for extinction. Get off that ship before it sinks.

If two people decide that they only want to be intimate with each other and authentically don't want to have any kind of physical connection with another person then I respect that. I feel that monogamous behavior that arises from 100% honesty and congruence (and, importantly, remains that way after the "honeymoon period") can fall under the vast umbrella of polyamory because poly is not about numbers…it is about love. If you want to love multiple people without sex entering the interaction then that is what is right for you. I only recommend that you don't project onto the future or equate your sense of security and happiness with the thought of things never changing. Go with the flow and keep being honest. Most of all, be honest with yourself because if you lose track of how you really feel and what you really want then you can't be honest with others.

If you try the polyamory lifestyle then you won't lose anything other than illusions such as guarantees about another's behavior. Unless another person has no free will, you can not actually control their behavior. If they are free there is a chance that they may love another person, and there's no reason to equate that potentiality with a threat to your wholeness. To fear this possibility is just a habit.

It seems that at this time the "swinger" community is much more well-established than the polyamory community. I see swinging as a transition between traditional relationships and polyamory. However, it still often values "coupleness" above all else, and often has many rules designed to limit the likelihood of expansive love or "losing" your spouse (thus implying you own them to begin with). I respect that swingers are breaking traditional societal norms, and I also have noticed that many people who join polyamory groups are people who have explored swinging but desire sustainable, contactful, expansive relationships. Again, if it is working for you, don't change it. But if you are not content, question the system in which you are choosing to exist.

Casual sex is not problematic. It is actually kind of strange that we have come to associate the pleasurable parts of the body with exclusivity. So many people enjoy being touched, hugged, massaged. But if that massage transitions to the breasts, or the genitals, or if a kiss on the cheek becomes a kiss on the lips, it also becomes "a problem." As we learn to accept more pleasure into our lives and become less attached to suffering we will begin to see that sensitive body parts are good. Sex need not require any kind of promise about what tomorrow will hold...only consent on the part of the two (or more) people involved.

Whether or not people are monogamous or polyamorous, the best method of determining whether or not a system is working is to see how those involved are experiencing it. If two people say that monogamy is working for them, then that is their truth. My sense is that for every person who is authentically content with monogamy there is at least one other who feels like they are settling but it is their only option...and have resigned themselves to live in fantasy and self-denial. If people are trying polyamory and suffering greatly, they must be honest with themselves about where they are at. The ego is a powerful little illusion, and to dissolve it overnight is a tremendous challenge. Be honest with yourself about where you are at in the process of working towards liberation from your ego.

At this time on the planet it seems that codependence is at an epidemic level. It is so common that it is accepted as normal. The media often displays codependent behavior as supposedly reflective of love. Similarly, jealous behavior is associated with love, even though it arises from fear. Just because something is seen as normal doesn't mean it's true. We are living on a planet that was once commonly viewed as flat. It is hard to go back to seeing Earth as anything but a sphere when you've seen images taken from space. And when you experience the liberation of compersion (the opposite of jealousy) it's hard to go back to believing that jealousy arises from anything that has to do with love.

Along the path of exploring who you are in relation to others, try to not judge. Remember that they are doing the best they can and anyone else's ego is just as ridiculous as your own. There is no need to judge another, and if you find yourself judging another, question yourself: How does this relate to me? What aspect of myself am I not comfortable with that leads me towards the judgment of another? Judgment can be utilized as part of your process of self-awareness.

If you are polyamorous, it doesn't matter whether or not you have zero, one, two, or more lovers. Polyamory is a philosophy that is about non-possessive love. Embracing this philosophy is non-quantitative and arises from a desire to experience the giving and receiving of love without conditions.

If you want peace, you will want to let go of controlling relationships. If you cling to controlling others you can almost guarantee that you will not find peace. There may be brief moments during which people are playing the role you would prefer that they play, but invariably they will eventually be themselves, and so it is best to just let go.

Time is often the variable that determines whether or not we see ourselves as monogamous or polyamorous. Look at the following two examples:

1. You date someone for a year. You then date someone else for a year. Then you start dating the first person again. You see yourself as monogamous.

2. You spend a day with a lover. You spend the next day with another lover. You then spend the next day with the first lover. You see yourself as polyamorous.

So time becomes a big variable. Yet many believe that time is ultimately an illusion. Attachment to the time we are with one person seems to arise from confusion. In our quantitative society, longer is better. Supposedly, being with one person for fifty years is wonderful. Of course if you know a miserable couple who've punished themselves and each other for half a century you may question this perception.

Nonjudgment in a relationship is an important aspect of what makes it work. The ego is tempted to judge constantly and assess whether or not another's behavior is benefiting one's self. Of course the ego is only interested in whether or not it is gaining strength, not about the evolution of one's true self. The ego likes control, power, attachment, guarantees. These are the illusions that keep it around.

We are powerful spirits in a body that has tendencies that for much of history have controlled human behavior. One of these tendencies is the sociobiologically driven urge to mate. We are "programmed" to act is if the only way we can perpetuate ourselves is through creating offspring. This leads to a lot of unconscious behavior that can be used by the ego to justify owning your sexual partner. This tendency is perpetuated in mainstream society with the subjective beliefs about monogamy and the traditional "family unit" being inherently good. Simply being aware of these influences helps you to transcend them.

Four spiritual concepts which can be found in various forms cross-culturally are nonjudgment, forgiveness, non-attachment and compassion. Polyamory offers many opportunities to practice these ideas. In a traditional monogamous relationship you are typically given societal "permission" to:
1. Judge your lover's desires towards others.
2. Not forgive any "straying" or "cheating" behavior.
3. Attach your sense of wholeness to the other's behavior.
4. Show compassion unless their behavior threatens your sense of safety.

Of course, anyone can practice these four spiritual concepts regardless of whether or not they identify themselves as polyamorous or monogamous. My goal is to help others become conscious of how society's message about what is "right" behavior can stand in the way of these underlying values.

Conscious hedonism is a method of living that will most likely increase in prevalence in the future. Much of the world is stuck in fear, but as the fear lifts, pleasure and joy will become more predominant on the planet. Hedonism is the pursuit of pleasure. Combined with consciousness, the pursuit of pleasure can be both responsible and harmless to others. If it feels good to have more than one friend, and it feels good to be in love, wouldn't it feel good to love more than one person? Polyamory opens the door to this love of many. If you are ready to walk through the door and risk letting go of control you will most likely learn a great deal about yourself and experience an amazing adventure.

As you travel along the path, make sure that you don't "bark up the wrong tree." In other words, don't look for a connection where it does not exist. This is self-punishing. Polyamory is in the cultural minority at this time. When accepting that your values are different than mainstream society's, you can reduce a lot of your suffering by not expecting to find polyamorous lovers in traditional dating realms. At least not right now.

A question that comes up for many people who are realizing they want to explore polyamory is "What will others say?" Depending on how you phrase it, you may be surprised about how accepting others can be. You may find that some people aren't ready to know about this aspect of your life in an accepting way. It's your right to reveal who you are at your own pace.

Throughout your journey, try to stay focused upon finding peace in yourself. It is easy to get lost in the vision of a happy polyamorous community living in harmony with nature, experiencing abundant joy and pleasure together, and all of that good stuff. However, you must be able to be content with yourself during the process. If you put happiness "out there" then you will be missing out on the peace that exists in the present. Take pleasure in the process of defining who you are with honesty and integrity. When you know your true identity you may carry the power of your truth wherever you go.

4

Accepting Acceptance

When we are young it is rare to feel fully accepted. Parents and other authority figures are seen as all-powerful, and often correct our behavior so that we remain safe from harm.

Sometimes their correction is helpful, such as when we are wandering out into the street. Sometimes it is not very helpful at all, such as when we are told that we shouldn't pursue our passion because it is irresponsible, or if we are forced to take lessons in something that doesn't interest us at all.

This parent-child control-based dynamic often continues into our relationships as adults. Many people feel that they can't be fully accepted, that love is conditional, and that being controlled is part of being loved.

Polyamory involves the risk of being fully known. Many people take the risk of being fully known by their friends, but not by a person with whom they are intimately involved. Threats to security arise because people often do not accept each other's sexuality unless it is a lie, unless it is a watered-down version of reality.

If you "only have eyes" for one person then you are less likely to be a threat to that person. Realistically, it is common to feel attracted to many people and to have the desire to be intimate with more than one person. How you handle this reality is up to you. In the realm of monogamy it is commonplace to keep truth hidden so as to not threaten your lover. Therefore you end up being fully known by friends but are a stranger to your lovers.

This creates an imbalance. Friends become more close to you than they are to your lover because they know your secrets. You may want friends to stay away from your lover and this would be one way to accomplish that goal…create a secretive world which they can not share with your lover.

Ideally, we can be transparent with each other so these artificial barriers need not exist. We all deeply desire to be loved for who we are. However, one of the greatest challenges to that goal is risking being known. If you don't risk telling your lover who you are, you won't feel accepted. If you feel guilty, you may tell yourself that you're not okay the way you are. Nevertheless, you are fine the way you are…and you are capable of finding others who accept you, including your sexual thoughts and behaviors. The first step, however, is up to you. You will not find acceptance without taking the risk of being known.

It would be useful to become conscious of your guilt. If you understand your guilt you may be less likely to perpetuate it by creating secretive situations. The Internet has increased the ease with which people can have secret relationships, thus creating more guilt and distance.

It is my hope that we may all risk being known so we don't perpetuate a world of relationships which are incomplete, conditional and limited by fear. We deserve better. We deserve to accept acceptance.

"The idea that obligatory exclusivity leads to sexual sustainability is contradicted by its tendency to lead to the opposite result."

5

The Evolution of an Intimate Relationship

People have a tendency to make choices in their intimate relationships based upon a very limiting set of socialized rules and roles. I find it somewhat sad because our tendency is to be free. Nevertheless the norm is not founded in freedom, but in simplistic limitation. Here are the typical stages of an intimate relationship:

1. Have sex.
2. Live together.
3. Get married.
4. Have children.
5. Divorce or stay together until death.

The only room for creativity is in whether or not to stay together or in rare cases whether or not to have children. And of course monogamy is generally not only seen as normal but "good" and "respectable." What I find disturbing about the assumption of monogamy is that most people seem to give away their right to make choices about their sexuality to their partner, and would be open to varied intimacy if they only had permission. This need for permission seems to stem from a desire to stay in the familiar role of a child who is not responsible for their own decisions.

I desire to break out of this system and follow my own path. My resistance in the past has been that I knew my decision to break free would (for a time) reduce the likelihood of an intimate relationship with the majority of women (because the majority of women consider themselves monogamous). Many women and men tend to buy into the system of monogamy without questioning it. It seems that women have more greatly than men been socialized to build their identities around marriage and children, and have been socialized to believe that intimacy with multiple partners makes them "bad."

Our current relationship patterns are largely based upon the idea that we will live for about 80 years, and the notion that the best we can do to perpetuate our essence is to have children. As we come to realize our true spiritual power, including our ability to remain healthy, the need to break away from limitation-mentality and built-in decay becomes more important.

To break away from an old pattern, it is important to be able to envision a new one to take its place. Here is my suggestion for a new progression of an intimate relationship:

1. Learn to experience yourself as whole.
2. Let your lover/s and yourself be free.
3. Continue to love more.
4. Remain unconcerned about the form in which your love manifests itself.
(The order in which these occur is not important.)

There is nothing simple or secure to hold on to with this approach to intimacy. Unlike the 5-step norm I described above, this approach is non-linear. You can't assess "how well you're doing" based solely upon what is happening in the physical world but must examine what you are experiencing in your mind and heart.

If the 5-step norm doesn't feel congruent, attempt to break away from a need to "fit in." Be courageous by daring to walk your own path. You may feel alone if you look to the media or your environment for reinforcement, but ultimately you will find your truth within.

"We are all forgiven by the Universe yet have the hardest time forgiving ourselves. But when we forgive others we forgive ourselves because we know that we are all connected and can't fully love ourselves while judging another."

6

Awareness Via Judgment

One way to gain a better understanding of our deepest conflicts is to examine who and what we judge. If we judge another person it is likely that we are judging some aspect of who we are. Judgment on its own is separating, but if we examine our judgments we can become more conscious of our issues.

For example, if we judge people who have no money as "trash" we might actually be uncomfortable with our own financial past or present, and looking for someone else to be "better than." Additionally, if we judge emotional songs as "stupid" or "silly" then it may be that we are denying the vulnerable emotions which these songs address.

It is useful to make a list of all the people you have been telling yourself you don't like then specify exactly what it is that you judge about that person. Try to examine if there are repressed aspects of your personality that relate to these traits you don't like. For example, if you have written down that you don't like your Uncle Joe because he is a control freak, examine your own thoughts, feelings and behaviors in relation to control. Do you feel out of control? Do you secretly try to control situations? This is an example of how your judgments can arise from a place of inner conflict.

I believe that we all know intuitively and logically that the world would be a better place if everyone was free to be who they really are. However, we are deeply entrenched in a system in which we are not only comfortable with judging each other, but seeing this as normal behavior. Eventually we will have to deal with the fact that every human being is interconnected and our separation through judgment inhibits our emotional and spiritual growth.

Of course it is easier to say "do not judge" than to do it. We often find ourselves in social situations in which the norm is obviously about judging another individual or group. It takes a lot of personal strength to fight against playing along with this dynamic. The best you can do is decline to partake in the judgment, or possibly find something kind to say about the person or group being judged.

To be completely judgment-free is a challenging ideal, and there is no need to feel guilty if you find that you still have many judgments. Of course, you weren't born with these judgments. You learned them. You probably learned that some people in your life will reward you for judging people that they don't like. People raised in sexist, racist, or homophobic households are likely to have more re-learning to do than those raised by nonjudgmental people. Enjoy the process of awareness. You will find that letting go of the judgments you have learned will liberate you from subconsciously judging yourself.

"When we evolve beyond body shame we find greater joy in simply being."

7

Sex, Vulnerability and Healing

Sex with someone who can see you on the levels of mind, body and spirit is a vulnerable act. If someone is only capable of seeing you on the level of mind *or* body *or* spirit it is a relatively less vulnerable experience since you are less exposed.

If you are being viewed by another as *just* a mind, *simply* a body, or *only* a spirit then you are not being seen holistically, and are leaving aspects of yourself untouched.

To touch is to heal if the touch occurs without judgment. To be fully exposed, to be fully seen by another brings insecurities to the surface. Am I attractive? Am I intelligent? Am I spiritual? Sex without judgment with someone who sees all of you does not simply express in words that you are beautiful, it communicates on a deep level that you are seen and you are valued.

Why sex? Why not love without sex? Simply stated, were we not to manifest for the lessons of physicality we would have remained in the form of spirit.

A basic understanding of the history of human socialization is an understanding of body shame. Sex is capable of producing the highest form of non-substance related pleasure to the physical form. This pleasure heals the misconception that the body is bad, and helps to bring a return to the pre-shame state of balance between mind, body and spirit.

If you are without a sex partner or sex partners, heal with yourself. Experience self-pleasuring through fantasy without shame or repression. Allow yourself to surrender to the moment. You do not need anyone else to experience your wholeness. Vulnerable sexuality is a pathway to healing but you do not need another person to heal your mind, body and spirit. You need only to practice the lessons of openness, truth and surrendering to the moment.

"When we battle against another we are projecting our internal struggle of yin and yang balance. Society teaches us that we are men *or* women but but our deeper awareness knows that we crave a balance of energy within that is ultimately androgynous."

8

The Integration of Yin and Yang

I am certain after the experiences I have had that there is a purpose to our life lessons. Many of my life lessons have revolved around learning the importance of my internal integration of yin and yang energy. Yin and yang energy is a concept which represents the dichotomies that exist in all, the "positive" and the"negative."

Much of the world believes that there is such a thing as "negative" in terms of there being an absolute wrongness of an act, or a word, or a behavior. However, when we understand our own freedom on a deep level, we feel completely liberated, no longer doubting ourselves or wondering if others know us better than we know ourselves.

Loving relationships seem in part to be about a process of becoming conscious of the games we play. When we become conscious of our games, we don't need to have dysfunctional relationships anymore. However, it seems as though most people are dying to know a love that is unconditional. And I do mean dying. The lack of unconditional love from ourselves and others actually harms the body. To experience love as based upon rigid conditions is destructive to our well-being.

Relationships have been largely based upon the idea that you need the approval of another whose values contrast with yours in some manner. In other words, having not internally come to an agreement between our own dichotomous viewpoints, we become conscious of our conflict through mate selection, and hope for their approval instead of our own integration. If we have understood our internal extremes and are ready to accept our true state of balance, then we no longer need to project these dichotomies onto the relationships we choose.

This harmony and self-knowledge is an experience which few human beings have had. People are capable of having positive relationships with each other that don't revolve around lessons related to their own imbalance (or the conflict

26

that is associated with such lessons). Furthermore, at this point we are able to share ourselves intimately in a spiritual form. It takes work to get to this place, but it is possible.

When we feel comfortable with who we are and no longer feel the urge to say, "Don't drink that or smoke that or touch her or him." then we simply feel the love which is present, and enjoy the moment. There is no need for rules, roles or expectations. Everything just is. And it's okay to love anyone. And when it's okay to love more than one person (since our nature is to love all people) it becomes okay to truly love ourselves and accept love without guilt or fear.

Why not strive to become someone who knows unconditional love within, between and without? There is no greater goal to achieve than love without any semblance of limitation.

9

Sexual Wake-Up Call

"Don't cry. Don't raise your eye.
It's only teenage wasteland."
—The Who

"Love my way. It's a new road.
I follow where my mind goes."
—The Psychedelic Furs

It's Time To Grow Up

Our world is deeply entrenched in sexual adolescence. There is much deception with ourselves and others, childish mind games, and a harsh cold war between the genders. It's tempting to simply give up on sex as a form of interaction, as many have. However, sex has great potential and can become a beautiful form of communicating our love for each other if we are ready to change. It is high time we grew up sexually as a gift for ourselves and for each other.

Core Truths

Among other things, I am a white, heterosexual male who lives in America. Though these demographics all put me at a distinct advantage in terms of economics and "power" they do not represent a sexual advantage. In this respect, I believe all ethnicities, sexual orientations, genders and cultures are suffering compared to where we can be. I will attempt to get to some core truths while recognizing that I am more capable of understanding myself and those like me than understanding a bisexual woman who was born and raised in Vietnam. I have faith that beneath our labels we are very similar in the sexual realm, and our inherited roles must melt away if we are to get to our true selves.

Orientation

My understanding of sexuality comes from a heterosexual perspective, though again, I feel there are core truths that transcend labels. The gay/lesbian population has the advantage of being better able to understand their same-sex partners unlike heterosexuals who deal with gender differences. Bisexuals have much to contend with and great rewards to reap…a great challenge with great potentials these souls have taken on for this lifetime. The greatest problem that the homosexual and bisexual populations face is the ignorance and judgment of the masses.

Bisexual females, however, seem in great demand. In part, this seems to arise from our patriarchal conquest fantasies involving polygamist domination. These fantasies shatter when men realize that bisexual women may not always want to be with them, are not likely to passively play out porno scenes, and are not likely to be controlled, if they have good self-esteem.

I believe that both genders are indeed drawn towards feminine energy in increasing numbers because there is a serious imbalance on the planet, which manifests as war and violence. The earth mother energy needs to arise and be honored in both genders or we will continue to suffer as individuals and as divided, fighting nations. I would like to see all nationalistic flags replaced with a symbol of balanced sexual energy such as the yin-yang symbol. If we eliminate the "us and them" mentality we can realize there is no one to fight against except our own self-imposed limitations. Sexual freedom is a fractal of the liberation we can experience on all levels.

Celebration Without Bureaucracy

I strongly advocate that people keep the government out of their relationships. People talk about health insurance benefits and so forth, but this kind of scarcity thinking keeps one stuck and miserable. If you trust that you can live your life with integrity, then there is no reason you will not manifest what you need economically to live in comfort. By becoming legally married, people introduce the government into their relationships which, I believe, in the future will seem extremely naive and unevolved.

Have celebrations of your love for those in your life. Have ceremonies if you wish. Celebrate the love of all of us and recognize the love that is there for everyone veiled by the ego. But stop imitating the past. Stop the surreal and unnecessary marriage between bureaucracy and bonding. The governments of nations are impersonal entities that arise out of the illusion of separation between the people of the world. Do nothing to taint your love.

The Soul Mate Myth

Believing that you can own another person will cause you great suffering. Believing that you have the right to do so will lead to a constant state of fear. Know that you are whole. Everybody says this, but if you have never lived alone, consider doing so for one cycle of the planet around the sun. See what you learn in each season. If you cannot live with yourself then you're in a constant state of dependence, which leads to resentment.

The ownership that arises from the monogamous mind-set leads to both subtle and overt violence. It also creates completely needless deception. Love is expansive. It is also natural to become intimate with those we love who are not physically repulsive to us. Look out everyone! You can't hold back the floodgates much longer. We're becoming too sensitive and psychic to lie to each other any longer. Our souls crave truth too greatly to pretend that we are only attracted to one person.

The soul mate myth puts the lives of so many in limbo only to await for an illusion that never comes. If one feels it is present, it is only a temporary high that after months or years of micromanagement becomes painfully disillusioning. This disillusionment is good; all disillusionment is good because only in the undoing of illusion can we get to the core of what is real. When we evolve beyond our illusions we are incapable of experiencing disillusionment. The ego has been burnt out from the pit of our minds leaving only ashes which dissipate to nothingness in the cool, gentle winds of truth.

Insane Gender Standoff

Women don't value having sex as much as men because it is easier for a woman to have sex. This statement is no more radical than saying a person dying of thirst in the middle of the desert values water more than a person drowning in a freshwater lake.

My first year of college was at a University with a 3:1 or 4:1 ratio of men to women. The women with sex appeal shut down their beauty because it was impossible to shine without being surrounded and engulfed by men. I learned about scarcity and how it drives men both to competition and alcoholism. We want to feel safe and loved, but in the absence of nurturing women, our lower chakra issues are often dealt with through alcohol. Meanwhile, men have cocreated a world in which women are afraid to shine because it may lead to being raped. Hunched over and trying to be invisible, they walk through the streets with no eye contact because men interpret eye contact as a sexual nod.

This system is insane.

Sleep Apnea

This book is a wake-up call. It is my wake-up call. It may be yours. You may already be awake. You may be comfortable in your sleep. You may believe in the media-perpetuated idea of soul mate as an elixir to take away your pain. You may believe that there's no problem with the system and it's just a matter of finding the right person. If so, you see the world as a bunch of partial people trying to complete each other without understanding what wholeness is, and you remain asleep. Perhaps you will not choose to awaken in this lifetime. I find that I can't sleep comfortably anymore beneath blankets of illusions and must awake despite the temptation to cling to the fairy tales about what love and sex should be.

You Are an Eternal Spirit Cell

You are your own soul mate. There are far too many lessons to be learned to expect one person to be the source of your ongoing evolution. It is tempting to simply try to stop this story…stop the growth…stop the change. Instead of seeing how we create the pain in our minds, it's very tempting to think that a soul mate will make everything simply stop and in this space we will find eternal bliss. However, it is as straightforward as math to understand that 0.5 remains half since two bodies never become one. It is simple math to know that we are all part of one interconnected web of spirits and to try to break off two spirit chunks does not add up to one.

The thought of you pairing up with another person and raising kids in a blissful state is deeply connected with images that will perpetuate the sales of minivans, toys, vacation packages and other distractions. Take back your mind and ensure your choices arise from within. You can be whole. Your wholeness exists in the recognition that you are an eternal spirit cell in the spirit body of all that is.

Letting Go of Possession

It is so very tempting to believe that jealousy is somehow connected with love. Jealousy arises from the notion that if someone enjoys apples they must stop enjoying oranges. Subtle competition between friends for the attention of a potential lover keeps us stuck in a primitive ape state that prevents our harmonious release from the hell of separation. Of course, if we release the notion that apples negate oranges and vice versa we eliminate the need for scarcity thinking.

Jealousy also stems from the notion of possession, which will seem bizarre, as we look back upon ourselves from an enlightened state. It will seem sad and silly to think that we used to say "my girlfriend" and "my boyfriend." It will seem pathetic that we used to so quickly establish ownership in social situations by introducing another human being as "my" wife/husband. It will seem equally ridiculous to look back upon the body language we used with a lover to communicate to everyone in our environment that our lover was "off limits" and any attempt to connect with our lover was grounds for violence.

Monkeys we were.

Sex Frequency

It is tempting to try to connect one's spiritual path to the absence of sex. This is leftover thinking from paths in which there was nothing better to do than to give up things that brought pleasure, as if suffering would be rewarded. This illusory thinking stemmed from a belief that God was sadistic as opposed to the culmination of all that is love, all that is true.

I once communicated over the Internet with a woman who was several years into abstinence and had so many years to go before she reached some rite of passage that would bring her greater joy. Of course, the power of belief can delude someone for awhile, but the absence of sex leaves one only as they are…happy or sad. If I told myself that avoiding eating blueberries for seven years would bring a great sense of peace and I achieved that goal I would probably feel good for a bit because I achieved this insane goal and would be proud of myself. However, there I would be…with myself as a happy or sad person…unaffected by what I once avoided.

There are two approaches to sex that cause great suffering: purposely avoiding it and trying to force it.

To avoid sex carries with it the feeling of being in control. It's similar to an eating disorder in which someone feels that their life is out of control, but they can at least control what they put in their mouth. Genitals replace the mouth in the avoidance of sex. There are many ways to justify the avoidance of sex, but the only thing that matters is that you are living congruently. If your mind is full of false ideas about what brings enlightenment (which I use as an abbreviation for the end of self-created suffering) then you will not become enlightened.

In forcing sex, we may create the feeling of being in control for brief moments of conquest, but beyond these moments are a complete sense of powerlessness. If you feel that you have to have sex once every six months then you will begin to panic at five months, and begin to force situations to avoid the pain that you've convinced yourself would occur in another month. You may falsely believe that mental health is associated with partner-induced orgasm once every "x" period of time.

The only thing that matters is that your mind is free of ego chatter and you are doing what you feel guided to do. Inner guidance seems like a bizarre concept reserved for saints and psychotics until you experience it. If I'm guided to have sex in this moment then so be it. If I'm guided to not have sex in this moment then so be it. To tell myself that I will not be having sex within the next month or that I must have sex within the next month is to pollute my clarity with ideas from the past. These ideas from the past that I implant in my brain cloud my ability to listen to what I am guided to do in this moment.

We have the ability to be spontaneous and free. Maybe we will laugh in this moment and perhaps we will fly. If we are listening to the wise voice within then we will always know what we need to be doing and saying. I can tell myself that I'd rather be doing anything other than writing a book, but I can't escape the omnipresent voice that says it's time to tap tap tap these keys and share these thoughts. And so it continues…

Uncomplicated Communication

Sex is communication. This may not sound very sexy but that's only because we've limited communication to words. Words are a temporary concept in our evolution. Eventually we won't need them because everything we need to say will be expressed on our faces. Complicated ideas in this complicated world need complicated communication. Sex is an opportunity to experience heaven right now. All it takes is a partner who is able to give and able to receive. Sounds easy enough, but until we surrender the need for conditions, it will be a long time coming.

In the heavenly state of sexual communication, we feel what our lover wants and give it without conditions. Back and forth our loving exchange continues free of self-consciousness or shame, each touch caressing away the pain of the past, and increasing the high vibrational state of vulnerability, defenselessness and transparency.

Classic methods of introducing conditions into sexuality include exclusivity and implied perpetuation. Exclusivity when applied to the paradigm of friendship illuminates its insanity. Imagine someone telling you they enjoy your friendship but would not be your friend unless you got rid of your other friends. This is exactly what happens when friendship becomes sexual and conditions arise.

This is a crucial point that must be examined deeply. The message that is implicit in this insanity is that the level of giving pleasure is directly correlated with exclusivity. If we hug as friends this feels good but not as good as an orgasm. Hugs can be shared but orgasms mean you get to own someone like a pet cat. Cats don't want to be owned but they'll play along to be fed, completely oblivious to your projection that you own that cat.

What is it about our body that we hate so much that the pleasure we can experience must come at some expense, some sacrifice? Of course, the way we are socialized to stop running around naked and stop touching our genitals or touching others' genitals is the seed of our shame. When we recognize fully how needless this shame is, we can release it and reexperience our body in a shameless state.

The cartoon animals we were raised with were either clothed or sans genitals. This is hilarious because humans are the only entities that can conceptualize body shame. Castrating cartoon characters attempts to get children to ignore these potential teachers we call animals. Watch a bird. Observe a dog. It has a comfort with its own body that you too can have when you know you deserve to stop hating the parts that are highly sensitized for pleasure.

Loverfriends

One common myth that keeps us sexually stagnant and stuck in old patterns is the idea that sex will ruin a friendship. Between women and men, women have sexual power (often more than they realize) in most cases and they are the ones that act as sexual gatekeepers in male-female friendships. If sex ruins a friendship then it is obvious that the friendship wasn't very strong to begin with. If the introduction of greater pleasure between two people creates a problem, this carries a discouraging philosophy: keeping things at a low vibration will help keep relationships going. Many people are much more willing to begin a new sexual connection with some-one who is obviously toxic for them instead of being intimate with a friend.

A friendship can feel secure and safe in its celibate state. Sex brings up emotions that can make one feel less in control. Well, control is an illusion anyhow so it's best to surrender when mutual feelings exist. If it is a one-sided attraction then it would be damaging to explore sex since it must feel congruent for both parties. However, it is easy to be out of touch with your feelings because you're so used to the role that you've been playing that you have a hard time envisioning it differently.

It is useful to be silent with your friend. Talk can keep you in your head and pre-vent you from feeling what is actually present. Try eye contact to see what is really there. It's possible to spend time with a friend for so long that you lose touch with what is going on in their eyes. Pay attention, as there is a strong connection between two people experiencing each other's eyes.

If you become sexual with a friend, it is important to not fall into any roles or patterns, or feel a need to define that relationship in traditional socialized terms. There is no need to try to figure out what will happen next or what this "means." Importantly, do not attempt to tell yourself the ridiculous message that sex ruins relationships. If you tell yourself this enough, you attract what you fear by mani-festing what you falsely believe to be true; thus making it true.

Friends often make great lovers because the heart connection is already present. You know, trust and understand each other. Fear not to enhance that intimacy. If your friendship is true and deep, it will take more than sexuality to threaten its sustainability.

Pleased to Meet Yourself

In case you haven't realized it yet, there is nothing wrong with masturbation. Those who understand sexuality understand that in having a good relationship with their own body, they can experience greater pleasure during sex with another person. It does not matter if you use fantasy, visual stimulation or no imagery at all. It only matters that you understand that you have the ability to give yourself pleasure. There is great symbolism in this because it is an act of self love.

If you enjoy pornography then it is important to be careful that you do not have subconscious guilt. It is important to realize that we are socialized to believe that every woman in an adult film is drugged and raped, which is not the case. One core spiritual concept that will liberate you and everyone around you is the realization that there are no victims (at a core level we create our experiences for lessons). Pornography may be an enjoyable way to learn about various forms of sexuality you may not have yet envisioned, allowing you to explore what excites you.

How much masturbation is too much? How little is too little? The answer to this is parallel to that which I've addressed regarding the frequency of sex. It's important to simply clear your mind and listen to your guidance…then do that which feels congruent. Given the amount of tension and frustration that most people walk around with, it's probable that you are not having enough orgasms. If you feel satiated, then congratulations…you're a rare bird who is obviously willing to nurture yourself.

Making a Mess

If we weren't so anal retentive (controlling and fearful of "making a mess"), then we would be more likely to be sexual when it feels congruent. For example, if touching someone's elbow made them orgasm, creating waves of pleasure, release and happiness throughout their body, and no bodily fluids were involved (no clean up), then we would be more likely to make each other orgasm.

It's a subtle energy, but because we are generally socialized to not "make a mess," it unfortunately results in a resistance to the "messiness" of sex. Not for all people…some people enjoy making a mess and I suggest that we all let go and get messy with each other.

These stains are not permanent or anything of which to be ashamed.

Sex is Dirty

As children, we are given the message that sex is "dirty." This is an interesting phrase to examine. How did the phrase "dirty" become negative? Dirt is of the earth. It's a big chunk of our environment and doesn't seem to be a bad thing whatsoever. If you think of sex as dirty then you are correct. If you think dirty is bad then you are wrong. Sex is dirty in that it is of the earth, it is of the body, of the material world.

Avoiding the material world does not bring you any closer to enlightenment. If you eventually transcend the need for food, water and oxygen, that's extremely liberating. However, if you try to skip ahead and not honor where you are at, then you will be starving, thirsty and gasping for air. Such is sex.

Beyond the Dyad

And now for a topic that elicits great curiosity and titillation: group sex. The most important thing to remember in this realm is that it is not helpful to either force or avoid these situations. There is nothing either magical or wrong with sex with more than one person at the same time. If it arises naturally, then so be it, but in such a dynamic there are many relationships involved (how A feels about B, how A feels about C, how B feels about A, how B feels about C, how C feels about A, and how C feels about B…that's six perceptions…and that's only a threesome!).

There is no need to try to force such a situation. This, like everything else in your life, will arise when it is meant to be, when you are ready for these lessons. The beautiful thing about this dynamic is that it offers opportunities for compersion (the opposite of jealousy) and is symbolic of the expansiveness and unity we can feel in our love for each other. Puppies huddled together understand how nice it can feel to share in each other's energy. Again, animals can be teachers because they have no shame (unless perhaps if we "beat it into them").

Filter the Information Society

Be aware of what media you take into your mind. There is a subtle brainwashing going on via music, television and movies. It's not some governmental conspiracy or anything like that…just a side effect of taking in low vibrational ideas. However, there are also mind-expanding songs, shows and films (I'm far from a "kill your television" person), so simply choose mindfully what you take in.

Love songs, for example, are rarely healthy. There seems to be an implicit agreement between the songwriter and the listener that enmeshment and neediness are not only good things, but necessary in love. We will surely experience greater role models in television shows and movies, as people show they're interested in new paradigm ideas about relationships. In the meantime, use your analytical abilities to observe the kinds of messages you are receiving from the media.

If the love song states that someone can't live without another person, look out. Beware of the television program that portrays a couple taking passive-aggressive jabs at each other for 95% of the show, only to have a "tender moment" as they look at their children sleeping. And be conscious during a movie that shows someone's quest for wholeness as it relates to their search for a "soul mate."

You're whole. Love is an expansion of your wholeness. Don't be fooled by any ideas that reflect less than this.

10

A Vision of Polyamorous Community

The following describes a vision of polyamorous community and ideas related to living effectively in this community.

People can feel more deeply secure in love that has no restrictions or conditions.

The primary paradigm shift which is occurring in this Information Age (in which so many vicarious experiences are available through the media) is discontentment with fantasy arising from a desire for real experience. A belief in deservedness creates the necessary readiness for manifesting authentic experience.

Spiritual practice is seen as occurring in diverse, fluid ways. Orientation and affiliation are not important. Living congruently is the central focus.

People do not own each other in any manner.

The desire to form a possessive bond arises in part from "body identification" and the ingrained belief that breeding is your path to immortality (through passing on a portion of your genes). In reality you are immortal and will stay in this form as long as is necessary for what you came here to do, and need not experience "death" as it is traditionally defined. Instead, increasing congruent experience and living in harmony with spiritual laws will help you interconnect the material and spiritual realms until they merge seamlessly.

The purpose of this community is healing, personal evolution and modeling a noncompetitive way of living.

There is no hierarchy of importance amongst members of this community or between this community and others.

Not everyone will feel interested in this vision in this lifetime. Ineffective love strategies are required until they are fully understood by the individual gaining these lessons.

Successful members of such a community will be effective communicators capable of being comfortably present with authentic contact.

To be fully present in such a community, many will have to go through disillusionment regarding what the socialized world teaches and offers. Layers of "false self" will have to peel away.

The underlying values are peace, unconditional love, harmony, joy, healing, personal and societal evolution, abundance, transcendence of shame, etc.

Community need not be geographically centralized (people don't need to live in a centralized "commune" such as a big house or shared land). Some members may choose to own land that can be used for healing and recreational purposes.

Some people who desire this kind of love may currently feel angry, frustrated, uninspired and disinterested in relation to traditional love styles. This stems from an internal emotional communication from within that a change is required for happiness.

It may be tempting to look to the past to find experiences that approximated what you currently want, and to then attempt to recreate those experiences with the same individuals. Unless you and/or them have realistically changed in some profound way it is likely that attempting new experiences with them will result in repetition without satiation.

If you have children, both they and you may benefit from being raised by a community as opposed to two parents who live with the child/ren (which often eventually leads to one parent living with the child/ren if the parents separate). A community setting can benefit a child due to its diversity, and benefit the adults by allowing them the continuation of time for self-development.

Personal discomfort and discontentment often arises from attempting to find satiation within an incongruent system. It is not the "fault" of those in the system. If the system is incapable of transformation then it must be abandoned for one that is capable of providing comfort and contentment.

As you find others who share this vision you will recognize a naturalness and hardly any sense of struggle (if any) accompanied by a sensation of feeling "at home."

Physical attraction or non-attraction, unre-
solved past issues, and length of familiarity
can cloud your ability to see with clarity who
also shares this vision.

It is possible to live in this world without losing yourself in the values of the masses. Conscious, filtered media intake combined with listening to your inner guidance and interacting with like-minded people will help you stay focused upon your truth.

11

Love Beyond Form

One's culture tends to dictate the form in which sexual love takes. Generally speaking, sexual intimacy tends to fit into one of the three following categories:

1. Marriage (Husband/Wife)
2. Dating (Girlfriend/Boyfriend)
3. "Casual Dating" (Friend/Booty Call/Fuck Buddy/etc.)

The primary difference between #1 and #2 is a legal contract. The primary difference between #2 and #3 tends to be monogamy vs. non-monogamy. Since #3 is the least concerned with form it is also the least easy to label.

Polyamory is the beginning of an exploration into love that is beyond form. Although some in the poly realm choose to maintain roles (husband/wife/boyfriend/girlfriend), others are letting go of form and experiencing love that is beyond labels or roles.

Living in the present is a spiritual aspiration of many who are on the path to awareness. To truly live in the moment requires a tremendous amount of letting go. Some are willing to let go of projections about where they will live in the future, what work they will be doing, etc., yet resist letting go of the idea of who they will be loving (and, more importantly, who will be loving them).

Polyfidelity, primary/secondary partners, husbands/wives with lovers are all poly love styles that often still carry implicit assumptions about the form which love will be taking tomorrow.

From a spiritual perspective, we are in the process of evolving beyond our socio-biological drives as our primary motivators and moving towards a state of wholeness in the present. I ascertain that as our individual wholeness becomes a more important aspect of our identity, concern with labels/roles/form in relation to love and sex will peel away like dead skin.

Our shiny new skin will vibrate with a radiant sense of completeness and non-neediness. This is very attractive to others. It is tempting to see someone who is shiny and attempt to possess her/him, to capture that energy, to make it your own.

Such grasping leads to an unstable sense of semi-security that is always "threatened" by the possibility of abandonment. Neither monogamy or polyamory can liberate someone from dependence. Polyamory can become multiple-monogamy, multiple-dependence. There is no liberation except for the release from attachment to the form in which you experience love.

The ego will resist this "letting go" tremendously. If we are liberated from needing what we can't control then the ego is left with little leverage.

Kicking and screaming, the ego resists wholeness. Our sociobiological tendency to believe that wholeness comes in the form of partnership/coupling/tripling, etc. sneaks in and wraps us up in illusions.

Surrender into your own wholeness. Feel its warmth and genuine comfort. Question everything you've been taught directly or indirectly about love.

Open yourself to knowing only the form love is taking in this moment. When you know that you are fine regardless of whether or not you are in a sexual relationship with zero, one, two or more people you can feel free. Do not cling to what was or what is. Let it be, evolve and become.

Internet Resources

Spiritual Polyamory by Mystic Life
http://www.spiritualpolyamory.com

Spiritual Polyamory Online Discussion Group
http://groups.yahoo.com/group/spiritual_polyamory

Mystic Life's Writing
http://www.unification.com

References

The Who, 1971, Baba O'Riley, Who's Next

The Psychedelic Furs, 1984, Love My Way, All of This and Nothing

0-595-30541-5